F·E·A·R

ADVENT

THE SPY
MASTER

JAK SHADOW

Wizard Books

Published in the UK in 2005
by Wizard Books, an imprint of Icon Books Ltd.,
The Old Dairy, Brook Road, Thriplow,
Cambridge SG8 7RG
email: wizard@iconbooks.co.uk
www.iconbooks.co.uk/wizard

Sold in the UK, Europe, South Africa
and Asia by Faber and Faber Ltd.,
3 Queen Square, London WC1N 3AU
or their agents

Distributed in the UK, Europe, South Africa
and Asia by TBS Ltd., Frating Distribution Centre,
Colchester Road, Frating Green, Colchester CO7 7DW

Published in Australia in 2005
by Allen & Unwin Pty. Ltd.,
PO Box 8500, 83 Alexander Street,
Crows Nest, NSW 2065

Distributed in Canada by
Penguin Books Canada,
90 Eglinton Avenue East, Suite 700,
Toronto, Ontario M4P 2Y3

ISBN 1 84046 692 8

Typesetting by Hands Fotoset

Printed and bound in the UK by
Clays of Bungay

Contents

Introduction

Last summer you went to a holiday adventure camp. It was fantastic! Instead of teachers, real soldiers, explorers and athletes taught you how to do all kinds of things. You learned how to survive in dangerous lands, how to abseil down a mountain and how to crack secret codes. They even taught you how to track someone cross-country and how to avoid being followed.

On your last day at the adventure camp you were awarded five certificates and told that you were one of the best students they had ever had. You remember that final evening as if it were yesterday and now, with your dangerous mission about to begin, you replay every detail of the scene in your head.

After a last campfire and a meal in the open air, one of the sergeants whispers in your ear.

'Colonel Strong would like to see you in his

office. Please follow me. There is nothing to worry about; you haven't done anything wrong.'

You saw Colonel Strong on your first day. He is the officer in charge of the camp, a big man with a booming voice who is more than a little terrifying.

You cannot stop your knees from trembling, and your hands feel cold and clammy as you walk towards his office. You are wondering what on Earth he wants to talk about.

'My people have been watching you all week,' Colonel Strong begins. 'I know you have had a great time here and you've done extremely well. We are all very proud of what you have been able to achieve.'

'It seems that you are exactly what we are looking for. Sit yourself down and let me explain,' he says, pointing to the chair.

'The world is in great danger. More danger than you could possibly imagine,' the colonel continues.

Why is the colonel talking to you like this? He obviously has more to say so you wait for him to continue.

'My organisation is fighting a secret war against an evil alien genius.'

'But who is he and what does he want?' you ask

'His name is Triton and he wants to rule the world,' the colonel tells you.

Colonel Strong passes you a photograph of Triton. He is like nothing you have ever seen before. He has green skin, piercing red eyes,  pointed ears, a large nose and has strange lumps on his face. You would have no trouble in picking him out in a crowd.

'I have checked out your history and I have watched you all week. I know that you are loyal, honest and brave, but even so I cannot tell you any more unless you swear a solemn oath to keep this secret.'

You are not too sure what the colonel means, but you know he is trustworthy and you long to hear more. You swear the solemn and binding oath that you will keep the secret.

'I work for an organisation called F.E.A.R.,' the colonel continues. 'It is an organisation so secret that only a handful of people in the whole world know about it.'

'But what is F.E.A.R.?' you ask.

'F.E.A.R. stands for Fighting Evil, Always Ready,' the colonel explains. 'I don't want you to feel you've been tricked but this activity camp was specially set up to recruit the ideal agent,' he continues. 'We selected only children who we knew would be brave, strong, honest and, above all, quick-witted. We have watched you this week, and out of all the children, you are the one we have picked. We want you to become a F.E.A.R. agent.'

'Agent! What sort of agent? A secret agent?' you shout.

'Yes, a very secret agent. But I can only tell you more if you agree to join us. Or would you prefer it if we just forgot this conversation?'

'Of course I want to help, but I'm only a child. What could I possibly do?' you ask.

'All of our agents are children now. Triton has captured all our best adult agents but he does not yet suspect our children.'

'Why can't we just hunt him down and kill him?' you reply.

'I wish it were that easy. The world Triton comes from is millions of miles from our planet, but somehow he has managed to get to Earth. He has a time machine and he is trying to change our time and our future. We have to stop him. We managed to capture one of his time machines and we've copied it so now we've got one of our own.'

'You can count on me,' you say, smiling at the colonel.

'If you agree to become a F.E.A.R. agent you will begin your training during the school holidays. You have been sworn to secrecy, and must not tell anyone about the work you are doing. We will tell your parents as much as they need to know, but no more.'

Over the holidays since, your training has been completed. You have worked hard and learned much. You know more about Triton now, especially the fact that he uses a time chip to take him back to a particular time and place. If you can take it from him, or destroy it, he will have to leave. F.E.A.R. have made a chip locator and on every mission you will take one with you. It will help you to find Triton.

Now you are ready to begin your mission, but Colonel Strong's words are ringing in your ears: 'Remember you are facing a most dangerous challenge and an evil enemy'.

You wait for your instructions.

How to Play

Before you start, the colonel will tell you as much as F.E.A.R. know about Triton's plans.

This is not like a normal book. Each section of the book is numbered. At the end of each section you will have a choice to make. Each of these choices will send you to a different section of the book. You make the choices and decide how you are going to deal with Triton.

If you fail, your mission will end and Triton will be able to continue his plan to take over the world. If you manage to combat all of the dangers Triton presents you will defeat him and the world will be safe - until he strikes in another time and another place! The world needs you.

Your Mission

You arrive at the F.E.A.R. base just after dark and Colonel Strong welcomes you. He seems to be deep in thought and doesn't say very much until you are safely in the mission room.

'This is going to be a dangerous one. We need to send you back a few years. Our agents have picked up Triton's trail in London at the end of 1999. We are still working out what his plan is this time.'

'What could he want in London?' you enquire.

'Our scientists believe that he has kidnapped the inventor Albert Fudge. Fudge has disappeared and nobody has seen him at work or at home for over three days,' the colonel tells you.

'Who is Albert Fudge? And what could he possibly know that Triton needs?' you ask the colonel.

'All we know is that Fudge is a computer genius and that we've picked up Triton's signal in central London. I'll be able to tell you more when our agents have finished their investigations. We need to get to London and we'll send you back in time from our headquarters near Tower Bridge,' he explains.

The colonel shows you to a bedroom on the ground floor of the base. He tells you that you must eat a good meal and get as much sleep as you possibly can before you leave for London. You find piles of books about the city in the room and pages of information about what was happening there in 1999. It was the last year of the century and the world was celebrating the beginning of the next thousand years of history.

At breakfast the next morning the colonel looks very worried. Between mouthfuls of toast he explains.

'Albert Fudge was working on a super computer in 1999. His idea was to create a computer that could control all other computers.'

'So Triton has kidnapped Fudge and obviously believes that he can make a super computer. But what does he want to do that for?' you ask.

'F.E.A.R. has found out that Triton is living under the name of Gary Steel. He has set himself up as a criminal mastermind. His men have robbed several banks to collect money to pay for Fudge's experiments and equipment. We can only guess that Triton hopes to take control of all the computers in the world by forcing Fudge to make a super computer for him.' Colonel Strong

passes you a photograph of Triton in his latest disguise.

'What's so important about 1999? I know it is the end of the century and the beginning of the new millennium, but why has he chosen 1999?' you ask.

'Many computers had a problem understanding that the year 1999 had to become the year 2000,' he tells you. 'We think that as midnight strikes on 31 December 1999 Triton will turn on the super computer and take control of the future.'

After breakfast you walk to the helicopter pad and get on board with the colonel. In less than half an hour you are hovering over the centre of London. You land on a tall building near Tower Bridge. There are guards on the rooftop and you realise this must be the F.E.A.R. headquarters. You are escorted to a lift which takes you down through the building to the basement. As the door opens you see a large room in the middle of which stand a big glass chamber surrounded by computers, screens and switches. It must be the time machine.

'When you arrive in 1999 the basement of this building will not be in use. There are offices above and you must make sure you are not seen,' the Colonel warns you.

'Colonel, we've had news from Agent 47,' a breathless agent reports. 'Albert Fudge has left clues to help us find him and we need to work out the five letters of the password to his master computer. From what we understand Fudge won't give Triton the password and now Triton is starting to follow the trail, so there is very little time.'

'Splendid!' says the colonel. 'Where do we need to start?'

'Abbey Road,' replies the agent, 'in Studio 1'.

'What's Abbey Road?' you ask. 'Is it an army base?'

'No,' replies the colonel, 'it's the place where the Beatles recorded their music'.

'Who are the Beatles?' you ask.

'Let's just call them a 1960s boy band shall we?' sighs the colonel.

Now read paragraph **1** to begin your adventure.

The Spy Master

1

'As you know,' says the colonel, 'you must take the chip locator with you on your mission to help you find Triton. Apart from stopping him from carrying out his plan, you will need to take the time chip away from him so that he will have to leave 1999. You may also take one other item from the choice of three here.'

He leads you over to a table with three strange items placed on it. The first thing is a computer disk, which the colonel explains has a virus on it to destroy the super computer. The second thing looks like a watch and one of F.E.A.R.'s scientists shows you that it has a laser in it able to burn through metal. The third item looks revolting. It is just like an eyeball.

'This is an exact copy of Albert Fudge's eyeball,' explains one of the agents. 'If you hold it up to the security system you will be able to open the door with it because it will think that you are Albert Fudge.'

It looks horrible and squishy. If you wish to choose the eyeball, turn to **96**. If you prefer the laser watch, go to **90**. If you think the computer virus would be more useful then go to **84**.

2

You continue to walk up the staircase towards the clock room. As you reach the door you see that it is partly open and you look inside to see four of Triton's men sitting around a table. They are laughing and joking.

You have a choice. You can either try to fool them into leaving the clock room or attempt to get past them to explore it. If you wish to run past them, go to **88**. If you want to trick them then turn to **44**.

3

The door slowly creaks open and you see Triton standing beside a huge computer. Next to him is Albert Fudge, who is tied to a chair with a rag stuffed in his mouth, so he cannot help you.

'I thought I had lost you ages ago,' shouts Triton.

'I've tracked you by following Fudge's trail all the way here,' you say, 'and now your plans are finished.'

'I think not,' he replies, pulling out a sleeping dart gun and pointing it at you.

Will you try to knock him over before he can fire? If so, go to **48**. Or will you hide behind one of the computers? If so, go to **37**.

4

'Has Albert Fudge left a message?' you ask the mechanic.

'Albert who?' he replies. 'I don't know who you are talking about. Does he work here?'

It is obvious that the mechanic doesn't know anything, so you thank him and walk away. It is then that you see some of Triton's henchmen walking towards you. You have no choice. You must get into one of the capsules. Turn to **55**.

5

You can now hear a strange, whirring sound and different coloured lights flicker under the door. You have no idea what is going on inside. Then, suddenly, you hear a scream. Will you run outside? If so go to **64**. Or will you rush into the room? If so go to **70**.

6

Triton looks very confused, so he calls over one of the soldiers from beside the gate and begins talking to him. You try to move a little closer, but the guards surrounding Triton are looking into the crowd.

There is no way you can hear what he is saying. Suddenly the conversation ends and Triton has a smile on his face. He must have figured out the next clue.

Triton makes off through the spectators, surrounded by his men. You can see that he has a truck waiting for him. Will you follow Triton? If so, go to **41**. Or will you try to talk to the soldier and figure out what he told him? If so, go to **42**.

7

Only another minute or so passes before another tourist asks the policeman for directions. He opens the gate again to show the tourist where they need to go.

You walk quietly towards them and then slip around behind the policeman as he is looking at the tourist's map.

He hasn't seen you, but he could finish talking to the tourist at any second.

Will you walk slowly away from the gate? If so, go to **63**. Or will you run as fast as you can away from the policeman and go to **33**?

8

The capsule begins to rock and the men on the roof are obviously afraid of falling off. As suddenly as it stopped before, the wheel begins to move again and your capsule is heading around the wheel. Triton's men have climbed back inside the capsule behind you and are staring at you through the glass. At least while the wheel is moving they cannot risk climbing out to capture you.

You reach the top of the London Eye and see the city stretched out below. You still have no clue as to where you will need to go next. Then you notice something very strange. Now go to **20**.

9

You type in the password but nothing seems to happen. There is one last chance. Perhaps Albert Fudge will help you? He is tied up and Triton would not have done this if Fudge were helping him.

If you wish to untie Albert Fudge then go to **100**. If you do not want to risk untying him then go to **52**.

10

Now is your chance. You sneak carefully around the policeman and squeeze through the gate, which he has left only slightly open. He may turn and look at any second so you have to make a choice. You can either run as fast as you can away from the gate and go to **33**. Or you can walk slowly and calmly away from him and go to **63**.

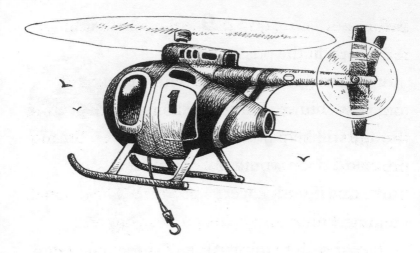

11

You run as fast as your legs will carry you, but the helicopter is always hovering over your head. Triton has spotted you. For a second he moves away and then swoops in towards you. Something seems to be tugging at your jacket, all of a sudden your legs leave the ground and you are flying in mid-air above the water of the River Thames. You look up to see Triton leaning out of the helicopter and laughing. He is clutching a knife in his hand and is cutting the rope that is holding the hook attached to your jacket. Suddenly strange shapes pass before your eyes and you feel yourself falling, falling, falling.

You find yourself on the floor of the time chamber and see Colonel Strong's face peering through the glass. Your mission is over. Strong promised that you would not come to any harm and he has kept his promise. The colonel opens the door and helps you to your feet.

'I was so close to catching Triton,' you tell him. 'I had found all the letters of the password.'

'You can return to 1999 again to have another go at catching Triton,' he says to you.

If you would like to try the mission once again, go back to **1**.

12

With great difficulty, you stand up and hear Triton shout:

'Get him! Stop him! He mustn't leave!'

You look left and right, hoping to find a safe exit, but Triton's henchmen, armed with sleeping dart guns, guard them all. You have decided to try for the main exit. Just as you get there, barely able to walk, one of the guards grabs you. You can see he has got earplugs in to keep out the noise that is sending everyone to sleep.

Will you struggle and try to escape? If so, go to **80**. Or will you give up and let the guard take you back to your seat? If so, go to **57**.

13

Holding the two buttons on your laser watch, you cut through the hinges on the belfry door. You then push the door in. Now go to **3**.

14

'Is everything ready?' shouts the colonel to all of the agents and technicians manning the controls.

The F.E.A.R. agents around the room nod their heads and you hear the time machine powering up to send you back to 1999.

'I'm told it feels a little bit like you're falling. You might feel slightly sick, but you won't come to any harm. Here is your tracker. Swallow this and it will tell us where you are and, most importantly, if you get into any real problems we can bring you straight back,' says the colonel.

'Just one thing, you're sending me back to an empty basement. Won't there be rats? I hate rats!' you exclaim.

'Just a few probably, but they'll be more frightened of you than you are of them.'

'One other thing,' he adds. 'We've already sent back a motopod. It is a lightweight, two-wheeled motorbike that is covered in a darkened glass pod so nobody will be able to see you when you're inside it.'

You shake hands with the colonel, then step inside the chamber and take a deep breath.

Suddenly, the chamber feels as if it is spinning around and around. The control room is swirling and fading and different shapes are appearing in front of your eyes. You hear a strange, whooshing sound, like a strong wind. You keep spinning and then you feel yourself falling. Now turn to **26**.

15

There must be 20 or more of Triton's men just metres from you. One of the men, who appears

to be the boss, is pointing in different directions.
The men split off from the group in twos and
threes and run in the directions he has ordered
them to search. Suddenly he points towards
you and two of the henchmen make straight for
your hiding place. There is nowhere to hide
and one of them sees and grabs you, pulling
you out into the sunlight. Strange shapes pass
before your eyes and you feel yourself falling,
falling, falling.

You find yourself on the floor of the time
chamber and see Colonel Strong's face peering
through the glass. Your mission is over. Strong
promised that you would not come to any
harm and he has kept his promise. The colonel
opens the door and helps you to your feet.

'You were getting close to finding the time chip,' he says. 'Would you like to try again?'

If you would like to try the mission once again, go back to **1**.

16

You are within a few metres of the bus when it begins to pull away. The men are gaining on you and you do not have very much time to make your mind up. Will you run after the bus and hope you can catch it before it picks up speed? If so, go to **23**. Or will you abandon the idea and run back to your motopod? If so, go to **36**.

17

With great difficulty, you push through the crowds in front of the gates of Buckingham Palace. Right at the front, surrounded by guards, is Triton. You are amazed that his green skin and large warts don't seem to shock anyone. Even his large ears are visible,

although he has placed a hat
on his head and is
trying not to draw
attention to himself.
Triton is carefully watching
the soldiers and seems to be trying to figure
something out.

You walk as close to him as you dare, hiding
behind a group of Japanese tourists who have
all got large video cameras on their shoulders.
Will you continue to watch Triton? If so, go to
6. Or will you attack him now? If so, go to **24**.

18

You begin your slow and steady climb up the
steps of Big Ben. It is very tiring and you stop
several times for a rest. Each time, you check
the chip locator and see that the
signal is getting
stronger. Just as
you sit down to
rest, you hear a

crashing noise. It is getting louder by the second. Something, or someone, is coming down the stairs towards you. Will you flatten yourself against the wall? If so, go to **91**. Or will you run up the stairs as fast as you can to find out what the sound is? If so, go to **83**.

19

You try to hide but Triton follows you.

'It was a good chase across London, but you lose,' he laughs. 'On the stroke of midnight my super computer will take over all of the computers in the world and no one can stop me.'

His finger begins to squeeze the trigger of the gun and suddenly strange shapes pass before your eyes. You feel yourself falling, falling, falling.

You find yourself on the floor of the time chamber and see Colonel Strong's face peering through the glass. Your mission is over. Strong promised that you would not come to any harm and he has kept his promise. The colonel opens the door and helps you to your feet.

'You were so close to the time chip,' he says. 'Would you like to try again and see if you can stop Triton this time?'

If you would like to try the mission once again, go back to **1**.

20

You look across the river and see one of the most famous sites in the whole of the city – Big Ben, the enormous clock tower next to the Houses of Parliament. There is something very strange about what is happening to the clock. The hands are going backwards! This must be your clue. Perhaps this is the next place that you need to visit?

The capsule slowly makes its way down the other side of the wheel until you have nearly reached the bottom. The three men following you are sitting in their capsule and the leader is talking to someone on a mobile telephone. Triton must now know that you are heading towards Big Ben, so he will be expecting you.

No sooner does your capsule reach the bottom than you are out and running away from the wheel. There is a road quite close and a bus has stopped. It has *Westminster Bridge* written on the front of it, so it is going in the right direction for you. Do you wish to catch the bus across the river? If so, go to **16**. If you wish to run to your motopod to cross the bridge, go to **36**. You must make your decision very quickly as the capsule with Triton's men in it has reached the bottom and they are running after you.

21

Triton must have been going to the London Planetarium. That was the direction he was heading in. Luckily you remember the map of

London from all the information Colonel Strong gave you to study. You decide that you must get there as fast as possible, so you jump on your motopod, with the plan to catch up with him.

The journey is quick and you think that Triton cannot be very many minutes ahead of you. You park your motopod behind some huge rubbish bins and enter the building.

At the London Planetarium you can learn all about the universe. The Planetarium shows a film of the planets and stars on a big, domed ceiling. It is just like watching the night sky. As you enter, a screening is about to start so you slip in with a group of tourists, taking a seat near the front. Without trying to draw attention to yourself, you look around the circular room. Standing off to your right, with a coat pulled up over his face, is Triton. You cannot mistake that green skin and those ugly warts. The lights dim and the show begins. Now turn to **43**.

22

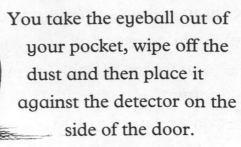

You take the eyeball out of your pocket, wipe off the dust and then place it against the detector on the side of the door.

There is a clicking sound and the lock opens. You stuff the eyeball back into your pocket and push the door. Now go to **3**.

23

You think that the bus will be the quickest way to get away from the three men so you decide to run after it. The bus is picking up speed and a crowd of tourists have slowed Triton's

henchmen down. Do you still want to continue running after it? If so, go to **59**. Or will you decide to hide in a doorway and hope that Triton's men cannot find you? If so, go to **66**.

24

You push through the crowd towards Triton and he spots you.

'Not you again. I thought I had lost you. Get him!' he shouts.

You try to make your way through the rest of the tourists to reach Triton. Many of the people think that you are part of a film and they are clapping and taking your photograph. They all think it is very exciting, but you know how dangerous Triton is. Three of his men block your path. They point their stun guns at you as Triton struggles away through the crowds towards his truck. Will you stay and try to deal with Triton's men? If so, go to **34**. Or will you try to work your way towards Triton? If so, go to **41**.

25

You spin around and run, not sure how you can escape the explosion. You reach the doorway then quickly look around to see Triton and one of his men fire the gun. It explodes in a puff of smoke, covering Triton and his henchman with dust and grime. You hear a heavy thump and the shell lands harmlessly at your feet.

Triton slaps his henchman around the head and thumps the gun with his hand. He then makes off in the opposite direction. Is there a clue here somewhere? You carefully pick up the smoking shell and see an eye painted on the side of it. What can this mean? You think quickly, trying to remember the map of London from your room at the F.E.A.R. base. It can only mean one thing – the London Eye. That's where you must head for next and the last letter of the password is an E.
Now go to **45**.

26

In 1999 the basement is filthy, full of rubbish and smells like a million cats use it for their toilet. There is a small canvas bag with a long zipper on the floor. You unzip the bag and inside it is the motopod the colonel told you about. It is no more than one metre long and has a cool control panel. You don't need any instructions, it is very clear what you have to

do, so you grab hold of the motopod by the handle behind the seat and look around the room.

There is no lift, just a concrete set of stairs leading to a wooden door. It doesn't open when you try the handle, so you push hard and it splinters down the middle then creaks open. You find yourself in a passageway with a set of double doors marked 'fire exit'. This must be the quickest way out. You push the handles down, setting off the alarm, and step out onto the street. The first thing to do is to get to Abbey Road.

You get on the motopod and press the button marked 'hood'. Two curved sheets of dark glass fold over your head. You press the 'start' button then punch in Abbey Road on the keyboard. The computer system shows you which way you have to go. You can see that Abbey Road isn't far from London Zoo. Abbey Road has given you the first letter of Albert Fudge's password, an $\underline{A}$.

Using your secret agent skills, you keep checking to see whether you are being followed, but you reach Abbey Road safely and are sure that you are not being trailed.

The famous studios are just ahead of you. You hide the motopod in a bush and then walk in. Before you leave your new vehicle you grab the remote control. If you need to get to it and cannot, then by pressing the remote control it will come to you. Will you ask the man on the desk whether Albert Fudge has left a message? If so, go to **46**. If you wish to look for Studio 1 go to **77**.

27

Triton has gone, but there must be a clue. Why did he start up the tank? What is important about it? You climb inside to see if he has left any clues behind. You do not have very long and the museum security guards are likely to be here any minute.

There is nothing of any importance in the tank, so you climb out, slide down the back and turn for one last look. It is then that you see an eye painted onto the back of the tank. What can this mean? You think quickly, trying to remember the map of London from your room at the F.E.A.R. base. It can only mean one thing – the London Eye. That's where you must head for next and the last letter of the password is an <u>E</u>. Now go to **45**.

28

You continue to climb and you can definitely hear someone shifting around above you. Looking up you see one of Triton's henchmen pushing a pile of bricks over the side of the scaffolding. They are going to fall on top of you! Just as the first brick falls you feel yourself falling, falling, falling.

You find yourself on the floor of the time chamber and see Colonel Strong's face peering through the glass. Your mission is over. Strong promised that you would not come to any harm and he has kept true to his word. He opens the door and helps you to your feet.

'I was getting so close to the time chip,' you say to the colonel.

'Would you like to return to 1999 and try again?' he asks.

If you would like to try the mission once again, go back to **1**.

29

You walk over to the main computer and stare at it for a second. You begin to wonder what is the best way to destroy the machine. Do you have the computer disk with the virus on it? If you have, then go to **62**. If you have not got the computer disk then go to **98**.

30

The tank is heading straight for you and Triton is inside, your chip locator is bleeping like mad. He opens the hatch at the top and shouts and points at you.

You run towards the tank and press the two buttons on your watch. In a second you have cut through its tracks and it is now spinning around and around, only able to go in a circle. Triton falls from view and you hear someone yell from inside the tank. He must have kicked the driver. With that the tank hits the wall.

In a flash, Triton and a man nursing a big bruise on the side of his head get out and run towards the exit. Now turn to **27**.

31

You decide to run, and as soon as you have got out of the room you begin to feel better. You hide behind a parked car hoping that Triton and his men will leave by this exit. But even after a few minutes no one has come out.

The door is still open and you decide to walk in. All you find is a sleeping audience and the large American lady is still snoring. Triton and his men have gone and you have no clue as to where he is now. You run out of the main door and look up and down the road, but you see nothing. You have lost him and lost your chance to find out what the next letter of Albert Fudge's password could be. Suddenly, strange shapes pass before your eyes and you feel yourself falling, falling, falling.

You find yourself on the floor of the time chamber and see Colonel Strong's face peering through the glass. Your mission is over. Strong promised that you would not come to any harm and he has kept his word. The colonel opens the door and helps you to your feet.

'I want to go back and try to stop Triton,' you say to him. If you would like to try the mission once again, go back to **1**.

32

The motopod zooms into view, weaving in and out of tourists and scattering Triton's henchmen. You dart out of the doorway and jump on. There is no time to punch anything into the keypad so you'll have to steer it yourself. You swing around, aiming straight for a bunch of Triton's men who jump to the left and right to avoid you.

You can hear shouting and sleeping darts whistle past you. Several of Triton's henchmen chase behind you, but you have a head start on them. As you reach the bridge you stop and turn around to see they are still following. You must keep going otherwise they will catch you before you reach Big Ben.

Just as you get onto the bridge you hear a whirring sound. A helicopter is heading straight towards you. It fires two rockets. One narrowly

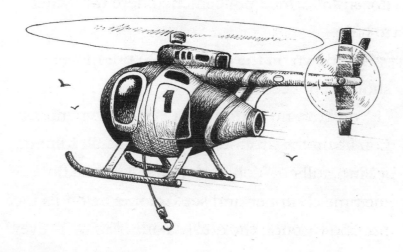

misses you but the other hits the back of the motopod. The vehicle is wrecked, so you jump off and look up to see that Triton is sitting beside the pilot. Will you try to hide? If so, go to **49**. Or will you run as quickly as you can across the bridge? If so, go to **11**.

33

The policeman hears your footsteps. He turns and shouts 'STOP!'. He grabs his radio and begins to talk into it. You continue to run towards Big Ben then you hear a siren wailing and, before you know it, you are surrounded by dozens of armed policemen. There is nowhere to hide.

'Lie down on the ground. Do not move!' shouts a policeman.

You have no option but to obey him and as you lie on the ground you feel yourself falling, falling, falling. You find yourself on the floor of the time chamber and see Colonel Strong's face peering through the glass. Your mission is over.

Strong promised that you would not come
to any harm and he has kept his promise.
The colonel opens the door and helps you to
your feet.

'You were getting very close to the time chip,'
he says.

'I had the password, and I think I was very
close to finding Fudge and the super
computer,' you tell him.

If you would like to try the mission once
again, go back to **1**.

34

You manage to run past two of Triton's men.
Suddenly, you feel yourself being grabbed by
the arm, but it is just an American autograph
hunter. You smile at him and continue to run
towards the last of Triton's guards. The tourist
has slowed you down and you see the truck
heading off into the traffic as three guards grab
hold of you. Triton has escaped. Suddenly

strange shapes pass before your eyes and you feel yourself falling, falling, falling.

You find yourself on the floor of the time chamber and see Colonel Strong's face peering through the glass. Your mission is over. Strong promised you that you would not come to any harm and he has kept his promise. The colonel opens the door and helps you to your feet.

'You were getting close to completing the password,' he says. 'Would you like to try again?'

If you would like to try the mission once again, go back to 1.

35

As you run alongside the slow moving truck, Triton is shouting out of the window. He grabs a pile of CDs and throws them at you.

'Do you want me to stop boss? Do you want me to deal with him?' shouts the driver.

'No you idiot, just keep driving. We've got the letter I and we are heading for the Imperial

War Museum. We're in a truck and he is on
foot. We'll get there first.'

Triton then realises that you have heard him.
Worse for him, you have ducked behind the
truck and jumped on board. You jump off at a
set of traffic lights just in front of the Imperial
War Museum and see the truck disappear
around the corner. Luckily, you've
remembered to bring the remote controller
for your motopod and you press it. In what
seems like seconds the motopod has squealed
to a halt in front of you. You may need
it later.

The Imperial War Museum
is a huge building with
an enormous gun outside
the entrance and you park
your motopod right
underneath the barrels.
You walk inside and
begin to wonder how on
earth you will find
Triton in such a large
place. Quickly, you
look at the signs, but
once again you feel as if
you are being watched. The same characters in
coats you saw hanging around earlier are
pretending to look at the pictures and exhibits,
but really they are watching you. Triton must
be here if his agents are.

You must make up your mind where to go.
Should you go and have a look at the tanks?
There may be a clue inside one of them. If so,
go to **97**. Or do you want to have a look at the

big guns? Perhaps the clue has been stuffed down one of the barrels? If so, go to **53**.

36

You zoom along the side of the river towards Westminster Bridge. Big Ben's clock has stopped. As you reach the bridge you squeal to a halt and turn around to see the three men running after you. You must keep going otherwise they will catch you before you reach Big Ben.

Just as you get onto the bridge you hear a whirring sound and look up to see a helicopter heading towards you. It fires a pair of rockets and you hear one whoosh over your head. The other hits the back wheel of your motopod, bursting the tyre. As the helicopter gets closer you can see that Triton is sitting beside the pilot. Will you try to hide? If so, go to **49**. Or will you run as quickly as you can across the bridge? If so, go to **11**.

37

You duck behind a computer just in time.
Triton fires his sleeping dart gun at you but it
hits the screen instead. The glass shatters and
he curses. He is trying to reload his gun. You
might have a chance to get to him before he
can reload. Will you continue to hide behind
the computer? If so, go to **60**. Or will you rush
at him and go to **73**?

38

A large black
metal gate,
guarded by a
policeman,
blocks your way
to Big Ben. It is
locked and the
policeman is standing
on the other side.

It would be
impossible to

climb the gate without him seeing you, but you need to get past him to reach Big Ben. You watch for a few seconds, not daring to wait much longer because Triton's henchmen are close behind you.

The policeman opens the gate to give directions to a tourist. You could try to sneak past him now while he is talking. If so, go to **10**. Or you could wait for him to finish and make up a story to convince him to let you through. If so, go to **76**.

39

You cannot remember the password, but you put the computer virus disk into the drive and press every button you can see. Nothing happens. The virus will not work because the computer has locked you out.

There is nothing else to be done. You

must destroy the computer yourself. You pick up a brick and smash the screen and then pull out the cables and throw the computer onto the ground. Then you release Albert Fudge.

'Thank you for saving me,' he smiles at you.

'Can Triton make this super computer again?' you ask him.

'Yes, I think he can, he has my plans,' he answers.

Suddenly you remember that Triton fell through the hole in the floor and he may have the plans on him, as well as the time chip. You run down the stairs and into the clock room, only to find the room empty. He has left a note on the table for you.

'Better luck next time. I'll see you again in 1999,' it says.

Strange shapes pass before your eyes and you feel yourself falling, falling, falling.

You find yourself on the floor of the time chamber and see Colonel Strong's face peering through the glass. Your mission is over. Strong promised that you would not come to any harm and he has kept his promise. The colonel opens the door and helps you to your feet.

'It seems we've stopped him this time. But we have to be prepared for him to try his plan again back in 1999,' he warns you.

If you would like to try the mission once again to see if this time you can get the time chip, go back to **1**.

40

'Honestly, I am telling the truth,' you lie to the policeman. 'My Dad finishes work in about five minutes and I've got to meet him at the top of the underground car park.'

The policeman looks at you, unsure whether to believe you or not.

'Alright, just this time,' he says, 'but make sure your Dad tells me next time. Go on, off you go.'

The policeman opens the gate for you. You thank him and walk slowly towards the entrance. You hope the policeman doesn't get into trouble, but you know that you must get to Big Ben and stop Triton. Now turn to **89**.

41

You reach the edge of the crowd just in time to see Triton's truck starting up. It cannot pull out because there is heavy traffic on the road. Triton winds down the window and shouts:

'You're too late, I'll get away and my men will deal with you.'

Several tourists who think you must be famous are following you. Just as one of them is asking for your autograph, Triton's truck lurches forward and joins the traffic.

You have a choice. You can either try to jump onto the back of his truck, if so go to **79**. Or you can try to run after it, in which case you should go to **35**.

42

The soldier is a huge man who is dressed in a red jacket, black trousers and an enormous fur hat.

'Excuse me, what did that, er, man ask you?' you question the soldier.

'Pardon sonny, what did he ask me? He just asked me which regiment I am in,' he tells you. 'It seemed to please him.'

'Which regiment are you in?' you ask.

'The Irish Guards,' he says, saluting you.

'Where could I go to find out more about the Irish Guards?' you ask the soldier.

'Um, let me think. Well, there's the army museum or there's the Imperial War Museum of course.'

That must be it. The Imperial War Museum. The letter I. That must be your next clue. Irish Guards and Imperial War Museum both begin with an I. You can add I to your collection of letters. Turn to **72**.

43

At first the film appears perfectly normal. Various stars and planets appear in the light show above your head. A man's voice describes the planets and then it cuts out and is replaced by a high-pitched noise. You begin to feel very, very sleepy. A large American lady has tipped her head towards you and is snoring in your ear.

Triton must be trying to put everyone to sleep. You don't have much time – you feel like you are about to drop off.

Will you stay, even though you know that you will fall asleep in a few seconds? Or will you try to leave? If you wish to stay, go to **57**. If you wish to try and escape through the main exit, go to **12**. If you want to try the fire exit, go to **54**.

44

Carefully, you pull a brick out of the wall and then flatten yourself into a space by the door. You throw the brick down the stairs and it makes a terrible thumping noise as it hits each step. The four men rush out of the room, straight past you and down the staircase. You run through the door and slam it shut behind you, pulling the two bolts across it to stop them from coming back up.

Will you search the clock room? If so, go to **56**. Or will you head for the top of the tower, the belfry? If so, go to **69**.

45

You run out of the Imperial War Museum and jump on your motopod, hastily punching *London Eye* into the keypad as you fire up the engine. The motopod screeches off at break-neck speed and very soon you see the London Eye, an enormous wheel built alongside the River Thames. It is nearly 140 metres tall, making it one of the tallest landmarks in the city. You remember from the books at the F.E.A.R. base that it was built to celebrate the millennium. In 1999 it isn't open to the public, and the capsules are full of workmen.

It is difficult to guess where to go from here. You already have five letters and this, the London Eye, was your final letter - <u>E</u>. But where will the clues send you next? You park your motopod as close to the London Eye as you can and then see that a mechanic has just come out of one of the capsules. You could go and talk to him. If you wish to do this, go to **4**. If you want to just sneak on board one of the capsules then go to **55**.

46

'Excuse me, has Albert Fudge left any messages?' you ask the man on the desk.

'What? Pardon? What did you say?' he replies. You have obviously woken him up.

'Albert Fudge,' you say. 'Has he left a message?'

'Yes, here it is,' he hands you a slip of paper.

The badly written note simply says 'Studio 1 Gary Steel'. Now go to 77.

47

As you begin your climb to the next capsule it begins to rain, making it difficult for you to hold on to the wheel. The three men that are following you seem afraid. You are so high up you do not dare look down. You reach out for something to grab but your hand slips. Then your right leg slips and you feel yourself falling, falling, falling.

You find yourself on the floor of the time chamber and see Colonel Strong's face peering through the glass. Your mission is over. Strong promised you that you would not come to any harm and he has kept his promise. The colonel opens the door and helps you to your feet.

'I found out the password,' you tell him. 'I was getting close to the time chip'.

He tells you that you can return to 1999 to try and stop Triton.

If you would like to try the mission once again, go back to **1**.

48

You manage to cover about half of the distance between you and Triton before he fires. The dart hits you in your shoulder and straight away you begin to feel very sleepy and your legs give way beneath you. Suddenly strange shapes pass before your eyes and you feel yourself falling, falling, falling.

You find yourself on the floor of the time chamber and see Colonel Strong's face peering through the glass. Your mission is over. Strong promised you that you would not come to any harm and he has kept his promise. The colonel opens the door and helps you to your feet.

'You were getting close to the time chip,' he tells you. 'You could try returning to 1999 to stop Triton.'

If you would like to try the mission once again, go back to **1**.

49

Just ahead of you a woman is sitting on a bench, eating her sandwiches. She has the most enormous skirt you have ever seen in your life. It is almost taking up the entire seat. Without thinking, you run towards her, pick up the side of her skirt, and duck underneath it. She doesn't even notice. You hear heavy footsteps passing you and shouts from the henchmen. They have lost you! You lift up the edge of the skirt and peer out to see them disappear.

As you emerge from the skirt, the lady sees you.

'Terribly sorry, I thought it was going to rain,' you explain. The woman just stares at you and continues to eat her sandwich. You run the rest of the distance across the bridge and reach the gates of the Houses of Parliament, where you see Big Ben looming up before you. Now go to **38**.

50

You run out of the Planetarium and head for your motopod, but you get the feeling that you are being watched. Several odd-looking people, dressed in coats with their collars up, are pretending to read newspapers, but they are actually watching you. They won't dare do anything with all of the tourists around, but you need to make for Buckingham Palace as soon as you can.

Will you drive to Buckingham Palace on your motopod, knowing that you'll have to leave it somewhere safe and approach the palace on foot? If so, go to **17**. Or will you jump on an open-topped tourist bus? If so, go to **65**.

51

The door handle is very stiff and heavy. Carefully, you turn the lock. You push the heavy door inwards and it creaks loudly, echoing up the staircase of the tower. It makes an even worse noise when you close the door, but at least you are now in Big Ben.

There is a sign at the bottom of the tower, which tells you that there are 290 steps to climb before you reach the clock room and 340 to the very top of the tower. There is no lift, so this is going to be an exhausting climb. Now go to **18**.

52

You decide that it is best not to untie Albert Fudge and instead you run downstairs to take the time chip from Triton. He is lying on the ground, moaning. You turn on your chip locator and run it over his body. His time chip is in his trouser pocket and you take it. Just as you do he sits up and makes a grab for you. Quickly, you back away and smash the time chip under your foot. His body flickers and he shouts:

'I can't believe you've beaten me! There'll be a next time.' His last words are hard to hear as he disappears.

You run back upstairs and pull out the cables of the computer, then smash it on the floor. Only when you have done this do you untie Albert Fudge.

'Did you get my plans? He's got my plans. He can build another super computer!' he shouts at you.

'No, I didn't know he had them,' you answer him.

'He won't need me next time, if there's a next time,' Fudge tells you.

At least you have managed to stop Triton from taking over all the computers this time, but who knows, perhaps he will return to 1999 one day and try again. Albert Fudge leaves the room and suddenly you feel yourself falling, falling, falling.

You find yourself on the floor of the time chamber and see Colonel Strong's face peering through the glass. Your mission is over. Strong promised that you would not come to any harm and he has kept his promise. The colonel opens the door and helps you to your feet.

'It seems we've stopped him this time. But we have to be prepared for him to try his plan again some other time,' he warns you.

If you would like to try the mission once again, go back to **1**.

53

You walk into the huge hall full of large guns. Triton is standing beside one of them. In his hand is a device that looks a bit like your own chip locator, except that it has a mini-satellite dish on it. This gallery is not very busy and you are still some distance away from him when he spots you. Triton's dish must be able to locate the chip you swallowed.

You can see that one of his men has knelt down beside the gun and is loading a big shell into it. It looks like Triton is going to fire the gun. He swings it around so it is facing straight at you. What will you do? Will you run? If so, go to **25**. Or will you try to hide somewhere and go to **87**?

54

The fire exit is not guarded, but the guards soon spot you and start running towards you, firing their sleeping dart guns. The darts whizz past your head, but you manage to dodge them.

You are feeling very tired and need to get out of the room as quickly as possible. But you do not have a clue as to where you will need to go to next. Will you risk stopping and looking up at the ceiling in case there is a clue hidden there? If so, go to **58**. If you wish to just run and worry about following Triton after you have got out, then go to **31**.

55

You manage to get into one of the capsules very easily and join a group of workmen and their families, who are snapping the views with their cameras before you are even a few metres off the ground. The capsule starts to climb slowly towards the top. Suddenly, the wheel stops moving. There is a terrible grating sound and the capsule swings a little under your feet.

You look outside and already the hundreds of people below look like tiny dots. Then you look at the capsule just behind you and see that the escape hatch has been opened and three men in coats are climbing out. You watch for another couple of minutes and see that they are clambering along the wheel towards you. In another minute or two they will be here! Will you try to open the escape hatch and climb out onto the roof of your capsule? If so, go to **95**. The other choice is to wait until they are on top of your capsule and then try to rock the carriage to scare them off. If you wish to do this, go to **8**.

56

There are cables running across the room and through the ceiling to the top of the tower. This means that if the super computer is here then it must be at the very top of Big Ben. There is nothing else of any importance in the clock room itself, so you must now go to the belfry door, up the wooden steps at the other end of the room. Turn to **69**.

57

You decide to stay and your head begins to spin. The light show is replaced by strange dots before your eyes. The only thing keeping you awake is the American woman's loud snoring in your ear. Her mouth is wide open and she is

making a noise like a walrus. You cannot stay awake any longer and you feel yourself falling, falling, falling.

You find yourself on the floor of the time chamber and see Colonel Strong's face peering through the glass. Your mission is over.

Strong promised you that you would not come to any harm and he has kept his promise. The colonel opens the door and helps you to your feet.

'I'm sure that I can catch Triton,' you tell the colonel.

'You can return to 1999 again and have another go,' he says to you.

If you would like to try the mission once again, go back to **1**.

58

You glance up and see very clearly the letter B with a crown over it, marked in the stars on the ceiling. There is no mistaking this clue. The B must stand for Buckingham Palace, where the Queen lives. So, now you have the letter <u>B</u> to add to the two other letters.

You don't have any time to hang around. Triton's guards are closing in on you and you must run. Turn to **50**.

59

Using your last reserves of energy, you sprint towards the bus and grab the handrail, pulling yourself on board. You look around and the three men are less than a metre away and running as fast as they can. You run up the stairs and sit next to a woman holding a baby. She turns and smiles at you and you try to smile back, but are worried that Triton's men have managed to get on.

Your worst fears come true and you see the first of the three men climbing the stairs of the bus. They sit down at the back because they do not dare attack you here. The lady with the baby wants to get off at the next stop, so you decide to join her. The men remain seated and you walk down the stairs, hoping that they will not follow you.

You are standing on the platform of the bus as it crosses the river when you hear a whirring sound and look up to see a helicopter heading in your direction. Triton is sitting next to the pilot. As the bus reaches Parliament Square and stops at a set of traffic lights, you jump off and run for the gates beside Big Ben. Now go to **38**.

60

Even with his fat, clawed fingers, Triton manages to reload the gun quite quickly. You can hear him laughing as he walks towards you.

'I don't think I'll hit the computer this time. This time the dart's for you.'

He stands over you ready to fire. Will you try to find somewhere to hide? If so, go to **19**. Or will you try to grab his legs and bundle him over? If so, go to **73**.

61

You punch in A, L, B, I, E and the door unlocks. Slowly, you push the door and walk inside. Now go to **3**.

62

The computer screen is flashing a message *Enter Password Now*. Can you remember the five letters of Albert Fudge's password? If you can remember them go to **68**. If you cannot remember them go to **39**.

63

You slowly walk towards the entrance to an underground car park that is just beside Big Ben. You take a quick look behind you and see that the policeman is still talking to the tourist. In a few seconds you will be out of sight. Now go to **89**.

64

Without looking behind you, you run along the corridor and towards the main door. Just outside are the bushes where you hid your motopod and you duck down beside them as you wait to see what might happen. You switch on your chip locator and hear it bleeping merrily. Suddenly it gets louder and then you hear a truck start up beside the building. Triton climbs in next to one of his henchmen and drives off. His green, warty skin makes him stand out a mile. You wait to see which way he is headed and then calmly walk back into the studios and head for Studio 1.

The room is empty except for cables lying on the floor. They are snaking across the carpet like the largest bowl of spaghetti you have ever seen. You hope that there is a clue left in the room to help you find the next letter in Albert Fudge's password.

There are several chairs arranged in a circle but apart from that there are no clues. Then

you notice something. Each
of the chairs has a star on
it. What does that mean?
Perhaps someone
who sat here was
a famous
musician? No, it
must mean something
else. Where in London can you
see stars? Perhaps at a famous
restaurant or a club? You spot a leaflet stuffed
into the side of one of the chairs. You pull it out
and unfold it. 'A journey for the 21st century –
visit the London Planetarium', you read. Aah,
you think, the London Planetarium! They
show the night sky full of stars. That's where
you must go next. The second letter of the
password is an <u>L</u>. Now turn to **21**.

65

The tourist bus is full of people from all over the
world and the tour guide, a small, bearded

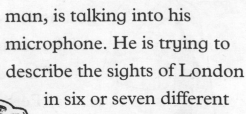

man, is talking into his microphone. He is trying to describe the sights of London in six or seven different languages. The trouble is that half of his sentences are French, with the odd German word in it and occasionally words that you think may be Spanish. Everyone is looking very confused.

The bus approaches Buckingham Palace and you can see the enormous building in front of you. You have arrived just in time to see the changing of the guard. This happens every day and there are thousands of tourists taking photographs of the soldiers. The bus is travelling very slowly and you can get off here if you want to.

If you wish to get off the bus, go to **17**. If you wish to stay on the bus, go to **81**.

66

You hide in a doorway, flattening yourself against the entrance. The three henchmen stop just metres from you and are all making calls on their mobile phones. In a few seconds several cars pull up beside them and dozens of Triton's men spill out of the vehicles and begin searching the area. You now realise that if you wait here there is every chance they will find you.

If you wish to continue to hide, go to **15**. If you wish to use your motopod's remote control and try to drive across the bridge, go to **32**.

67

You run down the wooden staircase and into the clock room. You can see the hole in the ceiling that Triton fell through – but he is gone! The door to the clock room is open and he has escaped. He now can return to 1999 whenever he wants to and continue with his plans to build the super computer.

At least he has not had the chance to carry out his plans, but he still has the time chip and perhaps one day he will return to 1999. You have done all that you can do and your mission is over. Suddenly strange shapes pass before your eyes and you feel yourself falling, falling, falling.

You find yourself on the floor of the time chamber and see Colonel Strong's face peering through the glass. Your mission is over. Strong promised that you would not come to any harm and he has kept his promise. The colonel opens the door and helps you to your feet.

'It seems we've stopped him this time. We

have to be prepared for him to try his plan
again back in 1999,' he warns you.

If you would like to try the mission once
again, go back to **1**.

68

You punch in the letters A, L, B, I, E and the
computer screen flickers and you have control
of the computer. You pop the computer virus
disk into the drive and press enter. Strange
signs and letters flash across the screen as the

virus wipes out everything on the computer.
The machine makes a terrible noise and
then starts to smoke. You have destroyed
Triton's program and now you can untie
Albert Fudge.

'Thank you for saving me,' he smiles,
rubbing his wrists.

'That's OK. Does Triton have any plans for
your computer?' you ask.

'Yes, he does,' Albert replies. 'He has a copy
of the plans in his pocket.'

You leave the room and run down the
stairs and see Triton lying on the ground,
moaning. You stand on his hand to make him
drop his pistol and just in case he has any
ideas, you shoot a sleeping dart into his
stomach. Kneeling down beside him, you
use the chip locator to find the time chip
in his trouser pocket. You then begin to
search his other pockets for the computer
plans. You find them in his coat pocket and
pull them out.

There is a box of matches on the table so you screw the plans up into a ball and set fire to them. All that remains is for you to destroy Triton's time chip. You drop it to the floor and smash it under your foot. Triton's body flickers for a second and, although he is sound asleep, he moans and then disappears.

You run back upstairs and see that Albert Fudge has been busy destroying all of the computers at the top of the tower.

'Is everything destroyed?' you ask him.

'Yes. The only plans left are the ones in my head. I think I'll take up a different job. I've always fancied living in Cornwall and growing organic vegetables,' he replies.

You say goodbye to Albert Fudge and no sooner has he left the room but you feel yourself falling, falling, falling.

You find yourself on the floor of the time chamber and see Colonel Strong's smiling face peering through the glass. Your mission is over. Strong promised you that you would not come to any harm and he has kept his promise.

The colonel opens the door and helps you to your feet.

'You've done it! You've beaten him!'

Everyone in the room is clapping and cheering. Your F.E.A.R. mission has been a success. You can now return home, pleased with your work, until the next time of course. Who knows where Triton will strike again?

69

The belfry door is locked. There seems to be plenty of security on the door to stop anyone from getting inside. If you have the copy of Albert Fudge's eyeball, go to **22**. If you do not have the eyeball then go to **94**.

70

You crash into the room and see dozens of
computers all hooked up together, with wires
running across the floor. You look around and
in the middle of the room you see a pod with all
of the cables attached to it. There is a man sat
in the pod. You recognise him instantly from
the photo that Colonel Strong showed you: it is
Triton. Next to each of the computers is a
musician playing an instrument. They all
look weird and as if they are under Triton's
control.

'An intruder,' he screams. 'Get him!' The
musicians stand up and
begin to advance
towards you,
looking like
zombies. There are
too many of them,
but you might have a
chance to get past them
and deal with Triton now.

Will you stay and fight? If so, go to **75**. Or will you run outside and escape them? If so, go to **64**.

71

The ladder looks safe and ropes tie it to the scaffolding. You manage to get up to the first level without any problems. You are already several metres above the ground, but you need to climb further. You make it to the next level, but then you hear a creaking sound above you.

Will you flatten yourself against the side of Big Ben? If so, go to **93**. Or will you continue to climb? If so, go to **28**.

72

Luckily you remembered to bring your motopod's remote controller. You press the button and in no time at all it has squealed to a halt in front of you. You jump on and punch *Imperial War Museum* into the keypad, then zoom off.

You arrive at the Imperial War Museum in double quick time. It is a huge building with an enormous gun outside the entrance, so you park your motopod right under the barrels. You walk inside and begin to wonder how on earth you will find Triton in such a large place. As you look at the signs you feel as if you are being watched. The same characters in coats are pretending to take an interest in the pictures and exhibits, but really they are watching you. Triton must be here.

You must make up your mind where to go. Should you have a look at the tanks? If so, go to **97**. Or do you want to have a look at the big guns? If so, go to **53**.

73

You catch him unprepared and bundle him over. He staggers backwards then falls heavily to the ground. For a second the floorboards

creak and then give way underneath him.
He falls through the floor into the clock room
below.

Will you run down the stairs to the clock
room and grab Triton's time chip? If so, go to
67. Or will you first destroy the super
computer? If so, go to **29**.

74

Two of Triton's henchmen are now on top of
your capsule. There is nowhere to run. The
third one joins them and he is obviously the
leader. He shouts something, but you cannot
hear him because of the wind. The other two
men move forward and grab you. Suddenly
strange shapes pass before your eyes and you
feel yourself falling, falling, falling.

You find yourself on the floor of the time chamber and see Colonel Strong's face peering through the glass. Your mission is over. Strong promised that you would not come to any harm and he has kept his promise. The colonel opens the door and helps you to your feet.

'You did so well,' he tells you.

'I had all the letters of the password, I was close to catching Triton,' you tell him.

Strong tells you that you may return to 1999 and have another go at catching Triton. If you would like to try the mission once again, go back to **1**.

75

The crazy musicians try to surround you, but you break through and head for Triton. He is collecting up equipment and has a computer disk in his hand.

'Too late, I've got it. And you know what that

means. With this disk I can rule the world,' he laughs.

You feel your arms being grabbed by the musicians and they drag you back, away from Triton, who is heading for a side door. Strange shapes pass before your eyes and you feel yourself falling, falling, falling.

You find yourself on the floor of the time chamber and see Colonel Strong's face peering through the glass. Your mission is over. Strong promised you that you would not come to any harm and he has kept his promise. The colonel opens the door and helps you to your feet.

'I know I can do better than that,' you tell him.

'If you would like to, we can send you back to 1999 to attempt the mission again,' the colonel replies.

If you would like to try the mission once again, go back to **1**.

76

The policeman finishes giving directions to the tourist and you walk up to him before he can close the gate.

'My Dad's a member of parliament. He told me to meet him by the car park,' you say. Luckily you have spotted the entrance to the car park and it seems like a reasonable thing to say.

'Really? You don't expect me to believe that. No one is allowed in here without a pass,' he tells you.

Will you try to convince the policeman that he should let you through? If so, go to **40**. Or will you wait until another tourist distracts him and go to 7?

77

You walk along the corridor and you can hear a horrible wailing sound, as if an animal has caught its tail in a door. As you pass the first door the noise gets louder, and then you realise that it is just some opera singers practising in the room. You continue walking along the corridor and there appears to be no one around. Finally you reach a door that says Studio 1. Underneath the sign is a piece of paper pinned to the door. It says 'Gary Steel Do Not Disturb'.

Will you wait and see what happens? If so turn to **5**. Or will you go into the room? If so go to **70**.

78

There is nothing you can do apart from smash up the computer and hope that Triton will not be able to rebuild it. You pull out the cables and throw the computer onto the ground. Then you release Albert Fudge.

'Thank you for saving me,' he smiles at you.

'Can Triton make this super computer again?' you ask Albert Fudge.

'Yes, I think he can, he has my plans,' he answers.

Suddenly you remember that Triton fell through the hole in the floor and he may have the plans as well as his time chip. You run down the stairs and into the clock room, only to find it empty. He has left a note on the table for you.

Better luck next time. I'll see you again in 1999, it says.

Triton has still got his time chip and he is right, he can return to 1999 at any time. At least you have managed to beat him this time and you have almost completed the mission. Strange shapes pass before your eyes and you feel yourself falling, falling, falling.

You find yourself on the floor of the time chamber and see Colonel Strong's face peering through the glass. Your mission is over. Strong promised you that you would not come to any harm and he has kept his promise. The colonel opens the door and helps you to your feet.

'It seems we've stopped him this time. We have to be prepared for him to try his plan again back in 1999,' he warns you.

If you would like to try the mission once again, go back to **1**.

79

You burst through the crowd and run towards Triton's truck. You manage to grab hold of the back of it and try to swing onto it. It is moving faster now and you lose your footing and slip and find yourself sitting in the middle of the road. An enormous red bus is heading straight for you. Suddenly strange shapes pass before your eyes and you feel yourself falling, falling, falling.

You find yourself on the floor of the time chamber and see Colonel Strong's face peering

through the glass. Your mission is over.
Strong promised that you would not come
to any harm and he has kept his promise.
The colonel opens the door and helps you to
your feet.

'I was doing so well,' you tell him. 'I nearly
had all the letters of the password. I know that I
can beat Triton if you let me return to 1999.'

If you would like to try the mission once
again, go back to **1**.

80

As you struggle with the guard you manage to
pull out his earplugs and he slumps to the floor,
fast asleep. The earplugs are revolting, they are
covered in yellow earwax and although you
don't really want to put them in your own ears,
you have no choice. The moment you do, you
begin to feel much better.

You decide to look up at the ceiling to see if
you can find a clue. Now go to **58**.

81

You decide to stay on the bus and try to pick out Triton in the crowd. You see him at the front, watching the soldiers. It must be them that will provide the clue. The soldiers are marching backwards and forwards, but not in a line or a column. They are marching in the shape of a letter I. This could be the fourth letter of the password.

You try to think. They are soldiers and the letter is I. What is there in London to do with soldiers that begins with the letter I? It comes to you in a flash! It must be the Imperial War Museum. That is your next clue and destination. Now turn to 72.

82

One of the tanks starts to move towards you. Triton appears from the hatch at the top and stares at you, then laughs. The tank suddenly swerves away and smashes straight through a wall. He obviously doesn't want to fight you

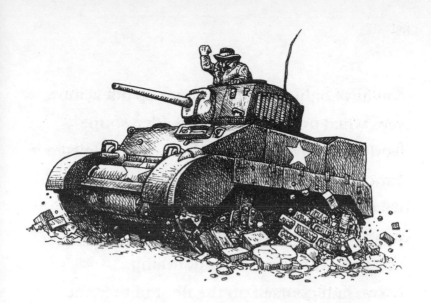

here and has more important things on his mind. You dive to the side to avoid the falling bricks and plaster and look up to see the tank disappearing through the hole it has made in the wall.

The tank has an eye painted on the back of it. What can this mean? You think quickly, trying to remember the map of London from your room at the F.E.A.R. base. You realise that it can only mean one thing – the London Eye. That's where you must head for next and the final letter of the password is an <u>E</u>. Now go to **45**.

83

You have only managed to get up a few more steps when you see a large, golden shape heading towards you. Each time it hits a step it clangs loudly. It is a bell. They have thrown a bell down the staircase at you. You cannot avoid it and just as it is about to hit you, you feel yourself falling, falling, falling.

You find yourself on the floor of the time chamber and see Colonel Strong's face peering through the glass. Your mission is over. Strong promised that you would not come to any harm and he has kept his promise. The colonel opens the door and helps you to your feet.

'Well done, you did very well,' he says to you.

'I found all the letters of the password, I know that if I was given another chance I could catch Triton,' you tell him.

If you would like to try the mission once again, go back to **1**.

84

You decide that the computer
disk with the virus on it
would be the most useful.
Providing you can get to the

super computer and pop the disk into it, the
virus should do plenty of damage.

'I'll take the computer virus,' you tell the
colonel.

'Yes, that virus will kill any computer,' the
colonel agrees.

You slip the disk into your back pocket and
pick up the chip locator. Now turn to **14**.

85

As you do not have the eyeball or the laser
watch, there is only one chance left. Can you
remember all of the letters in Albert Fudge's
password? If you can remember them all then
go to **61**. If you cannot remember them all then
go to **99**.

86

With an incredibly lucky swing of the rope you manage to hook it around the man's leg. You tug hard and he falls off the platform above you and is dangling in the air just metres above the ground. He is snarling and angry and you see him reach for his mobile phone, only to drop it. It smashes into hundreds of pieces on the ground far below. You only hope that he has not already told Triton that you are coming.

You climb up to the next level and see a window and carefully you climb in. You begin to walk up the stairs towards the clock room. The chip locator is now telling you that Triton is close. Go to **2**.

87

You duck behind a pillar and wait to see what Triton will do. He stands there for a second and then laughs before he rushes off towards the other gallery. You follow him into a large room filled with several enormous tanks. You cannot see Triton, so you switch on your chip locator. It bleeps furiously, so he must be in the room. As you look around to see if there is any sign of him you hear an engine begin to roar.

One of the tanks is starting up! Did you decide to bring the laser watch with you? If you did, go to **30**. If you did not choose the watch then go to **82**.

88

Without needing to open the door any further you squeeze through and manage to get halfway across the room before one of the men looks up and spots you. They jump to their feet, three of them head for you and one of them makes for the door. In a moment they have grabbed you and the third man has slammed the door shut. Suddenly strange shapes pass before your eyes and you feel yourself falling, falling, falling.

You find yourself on the floor of the time chamber and see Colonel Strong's face peering through the glass. Your mission is over. Strong promised you that you would not come to any harm and he has kept his promise. The colonel opens the door and helps you to your feet.

'I was getting so close to the time chip,' you say to the colonel.

'Would you like to return to 1999 and try again?' he asks.

If you would like to try the mission once again, go back to **1**.

89

In the safety of the entrance to the underground car park and out of sight of the policeman at the gate you take a short rest. Your legs feel very tired and you have hardly stopped chasing around and hiding from Triton's men since you arrived in 1999. At least you are safe here for the moment. Carefully you peer around to see if there is any sign of Triton and whether it will be easy to get into Big Ben.

You spot Triton's truck parked in front of the Houses of Parliament. No one is in it, so this must mean that Triton and his henchmen are inside Big Ben. The tower is covered in scaffolding and there are planks and ladders all the way to the top.

It is beginning to get dark and you realise that you do not have very much time left to destroy the super computer. Slowly you creep out of your hiding place and wait behind Triton's truck, ready to make your next move.

You switch on your chip locator, but it is only giving you a faint signal. Will you try the door to Big Ben? If so, go to **51**. Or will you climb the ladder to the first level of scaffolding and go to **71**?

90

The laser watch looks very useful. Not only does it tell the time, but it can also count down to midnight on 31 December 1999. The watch has an amazing extra, a red laser beam that can cut through almost anything. Locks, doors and metal should prove to be no problem with this device. The red laser is easy to turn on if you hold both of the buttons down at the same time, so there is no fear of you burning off your eye when listening to it tick.

'I think I'll take the laser watch,' you say.

'That's a good choice,' says the colonel.

'That should get you through almost anything.'

You fasten the watch around your wrist and place the chip locator in your pocket. Now turn to **14**.

91

You manage to squeeze yourself into a wide crack in the wall, just in time to see a huge bell clanging down the staircase, heading for you. It hits a step just beside you and then disappears down the staircase. You are safe. Now turn to **2**.

92

The wind is getting stronger at this height, making any movement on the wheel very dangerous. But you manage to climb to the next capsule. The people inside are shouting at you and trying to open the escape hatch to let you in. You look behind and see the three men following you close behind.

Just inside the escape hatch you can see an emergency button. This button will take your capsule around the wheel and stop it at the bottom. Will you press the emergency button? If so, go to **8**. Or will you try to make it to the next capsule? If so, go to **47**.

93

You flatten yourself against the wall of Big Ben just in time to see a pile of bricks tumble down from the level above you and smash against the scaffolding. Some of them tumble all the way down to the ground.

There must be someone up above you. There is a rope beside your leg, tied with a loop. Will you swing it up and try to grab the man with it? If so, go to **86**. Or will you continue to climb and face the man on the level above? If so, go to **28**.

94

You did not bring the eyeball with you, but do

you have the laser watch? If you have the laser watch, go to **13**. If you do not have the laser watch, go to **85**.

95

With great difficulty, you manage to unlock the escape hatch, open it and get out onto the top of the capsule. The three men are fast approaching, so you do not have much time. Will you try to climb up the wheel towards the next capsule? If so, go to **92**. Or will you decide not to risk it and surrender to the men? If so, go to **74**.

96

As long as you can find where Triton is holding Albert Fudge, the fake eyeball would help you get past any security system. It is a good choice, but it will leave you having to come up with some way of destroying the computer once you are in.

'I think I'll take this disgusting eyeball,' you say.

'That's a good choice. At least you can get past Triton's security system,' replies Colonel Strong.

You wrap the eyeball up in a tissue and stuff it into your pocket along with the chip locator. Now turn to **14**.

97

You walk into a large room filled with several enormous tanks. You cannot see Triton, so perhaps he did not come this way. You quickly look around to see if there is any sign of him, then you hear an engine begin to roar. One of the tanks is starting up! You switch on your chip locator and it beeps loudly to tell you that Triton is in the room.

Did you decide to bring the laser watch with you? If you did, go to **30**. If you did not choose the watch then go to **82**.

98

Still thinking, you walk up to the super computer and look at the screen. It is flashing a message *Enter Password Now*. If you can remember the five letters of the password then go to **9**. If you cannot remember the password then go to **78**.

99

There is no way in. You cannot get through the door. It is far too thick and strong for you to bash it down. Triton's henchmen are already hammering on the door to the clock room and in a few moments they will be through it and in the room. There is nowhere to go, no windows to escape from. You kick the belfry door, annoyed with yourself that you have forgotten the password. Suddenly strange shapes pass before your eyes and you feel yourself falling, falling, falling.

You find yourself on the floor of the time chamber and see Colonel Strong's face peering through the glass. Your mission is over. Strong promised that you would not come to any harm and he has kept his promise. The colonel opens the door and helps you to your feet.

'I was getting so close to the time chip,' you say to the colonel.

'Would you like to return to 1999 and try again?' he asks.

If you would like to try the mission once again, go back to **1**.

100

Quickly, you untie the knots holding Albert Fudge to the chair. You take the rag out of his mouth as he rubs his wrists.

'Download a virus! It's the only way to destroy the program!' he yells at you.

You run over to the computer and follow his instructions. The computer flickers as the virus takes hold of the machine, destroying the program.

'Does Triton have any plans for your computer?' you ask.

'Yes he does,' Albert replies. 'He has a copy of the plans in his pocket.'

You leave the room and run down the stairs where you see Triton lying on the ground, moaning. You stand on his hand to make him drop his pistol and, just in case he has any ideas, you shoot a sleeping dart into his stomach. Kneeling down beside him, you use your chip locator to find the time chip in his trouser pocket. You then begin to search his other pockets for the computer plans. You find them in his coat pocket and pull them out.

There is a box of matches on the table so you screw the plans up into a ball and set fire to them. All that remains is for you to destroy Triton's time chip. You drop it to the floor and smash it under your foot. Triton's body flickers for a second and, although he is sound asleep, he moans and then disappears.

You run back upstairs and see that Albert Fudge has been busy destroying all of the computers at the top of the tower.

'Is everything destroyed?' you ask him.

'Yes. The only plans left are the ones in my head. I think I'll take up a different job. I've always fancied living in Cornwall and growing organic vegetables,' he replies.

You say goodbye to Albert Fudge and no sooner has he left the room than you feel yourself falling, falling, falling. You find yourself on the floor of the time chamber and see Colonel Strong's smiling face peering through the glass. Your mission is over. Strong promised that you would not come to any harm and he has kept his promise.

The colonel opens the door and helps you to your feet.

'You've done it! You've beaten him!'

Everyone in the room is clapping and cheering. Your F.E.A.R. mission has been a success. You can now return home, pleased with your work, until the next time of course. Who knows where Triton will strike again?

The Emerald Pirate

Triton has become the Emerald Pirate! His crew are robbing and sinking ships, collecting a vast pile of gold and treasure, but why?

YOU are sent back in time to the peaceful island of Santa Diana, known to be the Emerald Pirate's next target.

Can YOU save the islanders, battle with zombies and put a stop to the Emerald Pirate's evil plan? Solve the puzzles and find the clues in this exciting adventure into a strange pirate world.

£4.99   ISBN 1 84046 690 1

The Space Plague

It is 600 years in the future and the inhabitants of Earth have started travelling to other galaxies.

Triton and his vile henchmen have infected the planet Rosetta, home to many humans, with a deadly plague.

YOU are sent forward in time to visit Rosetta with the only known cure. Can YOU battle with aliens to reach the distant planet on time? YOU are the settlers' only hope, but danger lurks everywhere! Solve the puzzles and find the clues in this exciting adventure into future alien worlds.

Published October 2005

£4.99   ISBN 1 84046 694 4

The Crime Lord

Triton has become the Crime Lord of London! His army of child thieves are robbing the capital. Even the best police detectives are powerless – they need help.

YOU are sent back into the foggy streets of Victorian London to solve the baffling case and bring Triton's grip on the city to an end. Can YOU discover Triton's secret lair? Can YOU stop him? Solve the puzzles and find the clues in this exciting adventure.

Published October 2005

£4.99   ISBN 1 84046 693 6

Fighting Fantasy™

Fighting Fantasy™ is a brilliant series of adventure gamebooks in which YOU are the hero.

Part novel, with its exciting story, and part game, with its elaborate combat system, each book holds many adventures in store for you. Every page presents different challenges, and the choices you make will send you on different paths and into different battles.

Magic and monsters are as real as life in these sword-and-sorcery treasure hunts which will keep you spellbound for hours.

There are over 20 *Fighting Fantasy*™ titles available.

Click on www.fightingfantasygamebooks.com to find out more.

Suitable for readers aged 9 and upwards

Fighting Fantasy™
The Warlock of Firetop Mountain

Deep in the caverns beneath Firetop Mountain lies an untold wealth of treasure, guarded by a powerful Warlock – or so the rumour goes. Several adventurers like yourself have set off for Firetop Mountain in search of the Warlock's hoard. None has ever returned. Do you dare follow them?

Your quest is to find the Warlock's treasure, hidden deep within a dungeon populated with a multitude of terrifying monsters. You will need courage, determination and a fair amount of luck if you are to survive all the traps and battles, and reach your goal – the innermost chambers of the Warlock's domain.

£4.99   ISBN 1 84046 387 2

Suitable for readers aged 9 and upwards

Fighting Fantasy™
Eye of the Dragon

In a tavern in Fang, a mysterious stranger offers YOU the chance to find the Golden Dragon, perhaps the most valuable treasure in all of Allansia. But it is hidden in a labyrinth beneath Darkwood Forest and is guarded by the most violent creatures and deadly traps.

To begin your quest YOU must drink a life-threatening potion, and to succeed you must find maps, clues, artefacts, magic items, jewels and an imprisoned dwarf.

£4.99   ISBN 1 84046 642 1

Suitable for readers aged 9 and upwards

Football Fantasy

Football Fantasy is a stunning new series of football gamebooks in which YOU decide the outcome of the match. YOU see what a footballer would see and make the decisions he would make.

Simple to play and challenging to master, every game is different. Learn the tricks and tactics of the game and lead your team to victory.

All titles £5.99

Thames United	ISBN 1 84046 598 0
Mersey City	ISBN 1 84046 597 2
Medway United	ISBN 1 84046 599 9
Trent Albion	ISBN 1 84046 590 5
Bridgewater	ISBN 1 84046 609 X
Clyde Rovers	ISBN 1 84046 621 9
Avon United	ISBN 1 84046 622 7
Tyne Athletic	ISBN 1 84046 596 4

Suitable for readers aged 10 and upwards